T0113946

GRADES 6-8

INCLUSION
ACTIVITIES THAT WORK!

Toby J.
KARTEN

For information:

Corwin Press
A SAGE Publications Company
2455 Teller Road
Thousand Oaks, California 91320
CorwinPress.com

SAGE Publications, Ltd.
1 Oliver's Yard
55 City Road
London EC1Y 1SP
United Kingdom

SAGE Publications India Pvt. Ltd.
B 1/I 1 Mohan Cooperative
Industrial Area
Mathura Road, New Delhi
India 110 044

SAGE Publications Asia-Pacific Pvt. Ltd.
33 Pekin Street #02-01
Far East Square
Singapore 048763

ISBN 978-1-4129-5234-7

This book is printed on acid-free paper.

08 09 10 11 12 10 9 8 7 6 5 4 3 2 1

Executive Editor: Kathleen Hex
Managing Developmental Editor: Christine Hood
Editorial Assistant: Anne O'Dell
Proofreader: Bette Darwin
Art Director: Anthony D. Paular
Cover Designer: Rose Storey
Cover Production Artist: Karine Hovsepian
Interior Production Artist: Scott Van Atta

GRADES **6–8**

INCLUSION
ACTIVITIES THAT WORK!

TABLE OF CONTENTS

Connections to Standards

This chart shows the national academic standards that are covered in this book.

LANGUAGE ARTS	Standards are covered on pages
1	12, 27, 56, 66, 68
2	12, 27, 56, 68
3	10, 12, 16, 17, 27, 54, 56, 60, 66, 68, 70, 71
4	10, 12, 16, 17, 18, 22, 24, 25, 27, 30, 51, 56, 65, 68, 70, 71, 78, 79, 80, 81, 82
5	10, 12, 16, 17, 18, 22, 24, 27, 30, 51, 56, 65, 68, 70, 74, 82
6	10, 12, 16, 17, 18, 22, 27, 30, 51, 56, 65, 66, 68, 70, 82
7	12, 17, 18, 22, 24, 27, 51, 56, 66, 68, 70, 71
8	17, 18, 22, 24, 27, 51, 56, 60, 66, 68, 70, 71
9	24
11	11, 18, 27, 30, 66, 68, 70
12	10, 12, 16, 18, 24, 27, 30, 51, 56, 60, 61, 62, 63, 64, 65, 66, 68, 70, 71, 74, 78, 79, 80, 81, 82

MATH	Standards are covered on pages
Numbers and Operations 1	34, 39, 41, 42, 44
Numbers and Operations 2	34, 36, 39, 41, 42
Numbers and Operations 3	34, 36
Algebra 1	41, 42
Algebra 2	41, 42
Algebra 3	41, 42
Algebra 4	41, 42
Geometry 1	46, 78
Geometry 2	44, 46
Geometry 3	44, 46

978-1-4129-5234-7

Geometry 4	44, 46, 78
Measurement 1	46
Data Analysis and Probability 3	36
Problem Solving 1	34, 36, 39, 41, 42
Problem Solving 2	34, 36, 41, 42
Problem Solving 3	34, 36, 39, 41, 42
Problem Solving 4	36, 41, 42
Communication 1	39, 56
Communication 2	39, 56
Communication 3	56
Communication 4	39, 56
Connections 1	34, 39
Connections 2	34, 39
Connections 3	34, 36, 39, 70, 78
Representation 1	36, 39, 41, 42
Representation 2	36, 39, 41, 42
Representation 3	39, 78

SCIENCE	Standards are covered on pages
Science as Inquiry: Ability to conduct scientific inquiry	56, 70
Understand about scientific inquiry	56, 70
Physical Science: Understand properties and changes of properties in matter	82
Science and Technology: Identify abilities of technological design	17
Science in Personal and Social Perspectives: Understand the importance of personal health	51
Understand risks and benefits	51
Understand science and technology in society	56, 70
History and Nature of Science: Understand science as a human endeavor	56, 70
Understand the nature of science	70
Understand the history of science	70

Introduction

Educators teaching students with exceptionalities in general education classrooms need practical tools and strategies to help ease their workloads, while meeting individual needs and standards at the same time. As difficult as it may sound, it is indeed possible to simultaneously embrace standards and differences, differences in abilities, learning styles, and intelligences. With the right tools, appropriate accommodations and modifications can be seamlessly and appropriately applied.

This book attempts to ease frustrations and replace them with proactive, research-based, effective strategies that apply across the curriculum. A multitude of activities offer practical ways to embrace educational standards, while differentiating the learning. These activities are not intended to replace your curriculum. Instead, they are designed to enhance your instructional repertoire through active learning environments that accommodate students' differing needs.

As an educator, you know your students best. The activities in this book can be adapted or modified to meet the needs of specific students in your classroom. In addition, this book includes teacher-friendly inclusion forms designed to simplify the inclusion process. Use them to help with documentation, communication, reflection, organization, and inclusion implementation. These forms help break through the educational jargon to provide direct, simple support.

As educators, meeting the standards is not the goal; *exceeding* the standards is the goal! Instead of thinking "My students can't do this," change your thought process to "*How* can I get them to do this?" Concentrate on strengths, not weaknesses. The eighteen activities are the backbone of the lessons offered in this book (see page 7). These approaches can be applied to a student with vision or hearing impairment, a student who has high cognitive needs, a student with behavioral challenges, as well as a student with more advanced skills. This book provides the "roadmap" to inspire the potentials and strengths of all learners and educators. Enjoy the journey!

Valuable Everyday Activities to Promote Inclusion

- Establish prior knowledge.
- Preplan lessons with structured objectives, allowing for inter- and post-planning.

- Proceed from the simple to the complex by using discrete task analysis, which breaks up learning into its parts, while still valuing the whole.

- Use a step-by-step approach, teaching in small bites, with lots of practice and repetition for those who need it.

- Reinforce abstract concepts with concrete examples.

- Think about possible accommodations and modifications that might be needed.

- Incorporate sensory elements including visual, auditory, and kinesthetic/tactile.

- Teach to students' strengths to help compensate for their weaknesses.

- Concentrate on individual students, not syndromes.

- Provide opportunities for success to build self-esteem.

- Give positives before negatives.

- Use modeling with both teachers and peers.

- Vary types of instruction and assessment, with multiple intelligences and cooperative learning.

- Make learning relevant by relating it to students' lives using interest inventories.

- Remember the basics, proper hygiene, respecting others, and effective listening, in addition to the "three R's": reading, writing, and arithmetic.

- Establish a pleasant classroom environment that encourages students to ask questions and become actively involved in their learning.

- Increase students' self-awareness of levels and progress.

- Provide many opportunities to effectively communicate and collaborate with parents, students, and colleagues.

Put It into Practice

Special education is at a crossroads—crossroads that have been repaved and redirected again and again. Why can't we just get it right? The answer is that perhaps there is no "universal right." We strive for universal rights in our world, yet differing political, economic, social, spiritual, and in this case, educational thoughts and policies abound. Academia conducts research, studies are carried out, and theories about best practices are born. The ultimate goal is to transfer the research into immediate practical benefits for students in that laboratory called the classroom.

The dilemma is that we live in a diverse world, one in which people have differing needs and abilities. Consequently, how could these theories then be universal? Is there such a thing as a universal lesson that meets the needs of all students? Can a student with severe cognitive impairments benefit from the same strategies as a student with more advanced skills? It is a challenge we all face in today's inclusive classrooms.

Instructional strategies are only beneficial when they match students' diverse needs. Administrators, educators, parents, and even students can become frustrated by the ever-changing legislative demands that although designed to benefit those with special needs, often create schisms among personnel at school, caregivers at home, and students themselves. Professionals need to both apply and raise curriculum standards making sure everyone is on the same page. The purpose here is to erase frustrations and replace them with research-based, effective strategies that apply across the curriculum, and that embrace school and home environments, and the potentials and strengths of all learners (Odom, Brantlinger, Gersten, Horner, Thompson, & Harris, 2005).

For example, students who have phonemic awareness skills are likely to have an easier time learning to read and spell than students who have few or none of these skills (Armbruster & Osborn, 2001). The National Council for Teacher of Mathematics says that students in grades K–2 must have standards that help them understand numbers, ways of representing numbers, relationships among numbers, and number systems. Do these standards apply for all or just some learners? Now that inclusion is the thrust, educators are compelled and driven to find ways to deliver the same standards to students of differing abilities. This needs to begin at these crucial early grades.

Educators can effectively instruct students of all abilities and potentials, having high regard for all, while embracing individuality.

978-1-4129-5234-7

Professionals can design lessons that include students with exceptionalities, such as those with diverse physical, behavioral, social, learning, and cognitive levels. The standards in general education must be accessible to those students with the most and least needs, and everyone in between! Classrooms must create a healthy environment that both recognizes and nurtures students' strengths, so they can flourish into critical thinkers, ready to tackle the many challenges in their academic future.

Students are assessed on the knowledge they gain. Schools are required to meet Adequate Yearly Progress (AYP) under No Child Left Behind (NCLB), with the Individuals with Disabilities Education Act (IDEA) still in place (Yell, Katsiyanna, & Shiner, 2006). Before alternate assessments are given, educators must look at the general education curriculum requirements and then make some decisions.

In the past, many learners with exceptionalities were often deleted from mainstream learning and placed in separate classes with lower requirements (Walsh & Conner, 2004). Unfortunately, this mindset then resulted in an adult population ill prepared to meet societal demands in the workforce and in social relationships. Today, special and general educators must collaborate to figure out ways that all students can and will be successful in school by creating and instilling high expectations, beginning with the early, formative grades.

Effective research studies and literature, with reference to specific instructional strategies, reveal the need for change (Harriott, 2004; Karten, 2005; McTighe, Seif, & Wiggins, 2004; Nolet & McLaughlin, 2005; Zull, 2004). Educators in the field are arduously trying to include students with special needs in general education classrooms. In this effort, researchers, administrators, parents, students, and teachers can all play on the same team. Delivering knowledge through principles such as step-by-step-learning while accommodating for individual differences and strengths results in strategic, meaningful, applicable, and long-lasting learning for all!

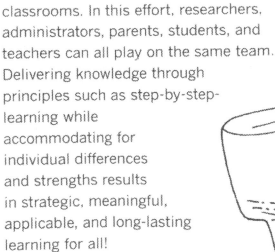

CHAPTER 1

Reading

Teachers sometimes assume that students possess prior knowledge and prerequisite skills in reading, and move on to the next topic. If reading skills are shaky, then well-planned lessons become futile. Some students, especially those with learning challenges, may have missed one or two crucial steps in earlier grades. They might never have broken the code and learned to just "get by" by memorizing words.

At this point, it's even more imperative to increase students' skills in deciphering words. It's equally imperative to be sensitive to the older learner, without singling out students as different or, in their minds, inferior, to their peers. Book choices and lesson designs in reading should be skill specific, yet age-appropriate. The following activities will reinforce essential reading skills and help to "fill in the gaps" students may have missed along the way.

Exploring Words

Word meanings are not random. If students learn how to break down words into parts, such as prefixes, suffixes, and root words, they will build an understanding of how words are constructed and how to make meaning of unknown words. The **Exploring Words reproducible (page 11)** helps increase students' knowledge of common prefixes found across the curriculum.

Invite students to look up words that begin with these prefixes. Then challenge them to connect these words to another subject area. Encourage students to keep this chart in a reading folder, adding words from their reading throughout the year.

Inclusion Tips

Encourage students to use electronic spellers, computer tools, standard dictionaries and thesauruses, textbook glossaries, and visual dictionaries.

Create a wall chart to display new prefixes. Introduce five new prefixes each week, or one per day. Remember to consistently revisit previously learned prefixes before adding new ones.

978-1-4129-5234-7

Exploring Words

Directions: Use a dictionary to find words with these prefixes. Write the words you find across each row. Then choose any ten words to write an essay about something you've learned in science, math, social studies, language arts, physical education, music, or any other subject you choose. Circle the words you used.

astr- (stars)			
bio- (life)			
circ- (around)			
dict- (say)			
equ- (equal)			
gen- (birth)			
geo- (earth)			
graph- (write)			
hydro- (water)			
mono-/uni- (one)			
ped-/pod- (foot)			
phon- (sound)			
photo- (light)			
strat- (sheet, layer)			
syn- (put together)			
tele- (distance)			
therm- (heat)			

Asking Questions

Reading involves more than just recognizing and pronouncing words. Some students can read words correctly, but have difficulty making meaning from or processing the information they read. If you ask students about a piece of literature, they sometimes have difficulty understanding the question or making meaning of your inquiry. The following activity invites students to think critically about text and develop their own questions.

Give students a copy of the **Asking Questions reproducible (page 13)**. Before they get started, model an example for the class and encourage students to respond with their own questions.

Inclusion Tips

Students with processing disorders and cognitive needs may require a modified assignment that asks them to just write one type of question. For example, they might concentrate on Main Idea or Details before moving on to Inference.

Stock a variety of books with assorted reading and interest levels in your classroom library.

Figuratively Speaking

Students with communication, learning, and cultural differences usually understand language on a more literal level. Figurative language can take on a whole new meaning. This is when direct skill instruction with figurative language is recommended. Practice with similes, metaphors, and idioms strengthens students' language skills and abilities. The **Figuratively Speaking** and **Figurative Language reproducibles (pages 14 and 15)** ask students to identify, illustrate, and explain some common idioms and create their own similes and metaphors. These kinds of activities invite student to flex their language muscles!

Inclusion Tip

Invite students to create an illustrated class book to which they can add newly discovered idioms, similes, and metaphors from their reading. Encourage students to periodically review the book and add to it throughout the year.

Asking Questions

Directions: After reading a story, write a question for each of the following. Then exchange papers with a classmate.

Main Idea: This is the most important idea of the story. Asking about the main idea might involve using words like *who, what, when, where, why,* or *how.* Find the main idea and rewrite it as a question.

Main Idea Question: _____

Details: These are facts that tell more about the main idea. This is a supporting detail for the main idea. Details may be specific names, dates, descriptions, or examples.

Details Question: _____

Predictions: Predictions deal with the future. Think about what might happen next in the plot or what might happen to the characters.

Prediction Question: _____

Inferences: An inference is looking beyond the written words. It is figuring out what the author hinted at, but did not actually say. Inferences must be supported by an example, a comparison, or maybe a connection between events and details.

Inference Question: _____

Sequencing: This is the order of events in a story. Words that indicate sequence include: *first, then, next, later, after,* and *finally.* These, along with other story clues, help you find the sequence.

Sequencing Question: _____

Figuratively Speaking

An *idiom* is an expression whose meaning is not literal, but stands for something else.

> **Example:** *I'm all ears* means "I'm listening very closely!"

Directions: Read each idiom. Then write what you think it means on the line. Choose your favorite idiom and write a paragraph that uses it as your conclusion.

1. It's a piece of cake! _____

2. Break a leg! _____

3. Don't spill the beans! _____

4. He's working for peanuts. _____

5. Don't beat around the bush. _____

Directions: Complete each of these idioms with a word from the box. On another piece of paper, draw or find magazine pictures or computer clip art to illustrate the idea of each idiom.

6. The untrained singer was a _____ in the rough.

7. A picture paints a thousand _____.

8. She's the apple of my _____.

9. Take it with a grain of _____.

10. It's raining cats and _____.

dogs
salt
eye
words
diamond

Figurative Language

A *simile* is a comparison of two unlike objects using the words *as* or *like*.

A *metaphor* is a direct comparison of two unlike objects.

Example:

clock

Noun/Concept

compared to

rooster

Different Noun or Concept

Simile: A clock is like a rooster that jolts us from our sleep.

Metaphor: A clock is a rooster, jolting us from our sleep.

Directions: Find similes or metaphors in a book you are reading, or create your own!

Word/Picture

compared to

Word/Picture

Simile: _____

Metaphor: _____

Cloze Exercises

Cloze exercises are activities that remove certain words from sentences or stories, and ask students to think critically and read context clues to find the appropriate words. This activity asks students to write their own cloze exercises to exchange with classmates. It encourages cooperative learning and reinforces reading comprehension and critical thinking skills.

1. Pair up students with partners to create the cloze exercises. Tell them to choose a subject such as social studies, science, math, language arts, music, art, health, or physical education.

2. Ask student pairs to choose a topic within that subject they have learned about this year. For example if they choose social studies, they might write about the three branches of the American government or presidential elections.

3. Have students choose vocabulary words related to their topic and write them down the side of a sheet of drawing paper. Then have them cut out the words to make word cards.

4. Then tell them to write sentences or a paragraph about their topic, using a vocabulary word in each sentence. This will be the "answer key" for the cloze exercise. This also gives students a chance to make any corrections to their writing before creating their cloze sentences.

5. Next, students create a cloze exercise by rewriting the sentences and leaving spaces for the chosen vocabulary words.

6. Have partners exchange papers and word cards with another pair of students. Challenge them to fill in all the blanks. Remind them to use context clues (surrounding text) to help them figure out which words go in the blanks.

Inclusion Tips

Some students may prefer to use word cards, while more advanced students can replace word boxes with page numbers from the text where answers are located.

Some students may need sentences and words read aloud to them, so you can determine comprehension rather than word identification level.

CHAPTER 2

Writing

Even though, by this age, students have been down the writing road, many of them still prefer it to be the one less traveled! The following activities offer inclusion activities that replace avoidance and discomfort with guided writing assistance. Technology, the writing process, strategies for purposeful writing, and writing planners help students down the path to not only writing well, but embracing writing as a lifelong way to communicate and express thoughts and ideas.

Computer Tools

Computers have become an invaluable resource in the classroom as well as in many students' homes. They are great resources for spelling, dictionaries, thesauruses, conducting research, and so much more.

Prepare several electronic documents with misspelled words, overused words, and some grammar mistakes. Put (*sp*) next to misspelled words, underline grammar and punctuation mistakes, and boldface "overused" words such as *said, happy, sad, big, little,* and so on.

Invite students to use the tools provided in the computer program to correct, revise, and improve each paragraph. Create a "tools list" and post it next to the computer, listing items such as *spell check, grammar check, dictionary, thesaurus,* and so on. Check the tool menu for other spelling and word options.

When students are finished with their revisions, have them choose one paragraph to expand. They can write one or two more paragraphs and then use the computer tools to revise those paragraphs as well. After the story or essay is complete, have students find an appropriate computer graphic to illustrate it.

Inclusion Tip

Students with visual impairments may need larger-sized font and/or screen magnifiers. If students have physical difficulties and cannot operate a traditional mouse, then investigate speech-activated programs and other options (e.g., foot-operated mouse).

The Writing Process

Writing is a five-step *process* that includes thinking of a topic, writing a rough draft, revising, editing, and then publishing. Give students a copy of **The Writing Process** and **ED's CAR reproducibles (pages 19–21)**. Read the text with students and answer any questions they may have. Reinforce the fact that writing is a *process*. The rough draft is only the first step in that process, which is then reviewed and revised. Invite students to put these sheets in their writing folders to use as references.

Remind students that writing is like talking on paper. They can express their thoughts and ideas through journal entries, short stories, plays, poems, newspaper articles, tall tales, and more!

Inclusion Tips

Have students mark every other line on their papers as a reminder to skip lines in their rough drafts. This leaves ample room for editing.

Review the meaning of the word *process*, comparing it to an artist's sketch that needs constant reworking.

If possible, consult with your colleagues about making cross-curricular connections that allow writing to be linked to other subject areas to increase comprehension, while developing higher level thinking skills.

The Writing Process

Good writing is a five-step process. Each step is important to making your writing the best it can be!

1. PREWRITING

Think about what you will write. Use an outline, graphic organizer, or list to organize your thoughts and ideas.

Here are some good places to find ideas:

- books, magazines, and newspapers
- conduct an interview
- electronic media (radio, TV, Internet)
- experiences
- movies
- music
- art (observing or creating)
- dreams

- memories
- discussion and brainstorming
- responding to literature
- role-playing
- research
- imagination
- personal interest inventories
- class interest inventories

2. WRITING

Use a pencil to write a rough draft. It doesn't need to be perfect. Just write down all your thoughts and ideas as they come to you. Let your ideas flow! Always skip lines so you can come back and make changes later.

3. REVISING

Writing means rewriting. When you're done with your rough draft, look back at what you have written. Think about how you can make it better. Ask yourself these questions:

- Is my writing clear?
- Does it make sense?
- Could I add more details to make my writing more interesting?
- Is the information in logical order?

Use ED'S CAR to revise your writing. Refer to the ED'S CAR handout.

The Writing Process (cont.)

4. EDITING

Now that you've revised your writing, edit it! Editing means looking for errors such as:

- punctuation
- spelling
- capitalization
- sentence structure
- subject/verb agreement

This step is a great time to share your writing with a classmate. Ask someone to read your writing and make suggestions for editing.

5. PUBLISHING

Your writing is at its best and ready for classroom publication! You can write your final draft neatly in ink or use a computer. Make your writing look as neat and clean as possible.

ED'S CAR

Expand
Write a simple sentence. Then make it longer by asking *who, what, when, where, why,* and *how* questions.

Expand this sentence: *The herbivores ate.*

- *Who* are the herbivores?
- *What* do the herbivores eat?
- *When* do the herbivores eat?
- *Where* do the herbivores eat?
- *Why* do the herbivores eat?
- *How* do the herbivores eat?

New sentence: *The frail, hungry deer nibbled at the tree's bark during the harsh winter.*

Delete
Take away extra words that say the same thing.

Delete some words: *Carnivores eat the bodies of organisms and they eat other animals.*

Hint: *Organisms are animals!*

New sentence: *Carnivores eat the bodies of other animals.*

Substitute
Replace words with more specific, interesting words. Look for overused words like *said, happy, sad, fast, slow, big,* and *little.*

Substitute and delete some words in this sentence: *The consumer consumed the food.*

Hint: *Who was the consumer? What food was the consumer eating?*

New sentence: *The bear slurped a paw full of fresh, raw honey.*

Combine And Rearrange:
Combine and rearrange the words in this sentence: *Omnivores eat plants, and omnivores eat animals.*

New sentence: *Omnivores eat both plants and animals.*

Transitions and Flow

Knowing how to create segues between paragraphs or ideas is key to making writing flow smoothly. One thought should flow logically to the next. To reinforce this skill, it's useful for students to have a list of transitional words and phrases as a reference when writing.

Give students a copy of the **Make It Flow reproducible (page 23)**. Through repeated practice, using transitions will become second nature in the writing process. Tell students to keep the transitional words list in their writing folders for future reference.

Invite students to choose one topic to write about, such as the Magna Carta or the American Civil War. Provide them with the following facts about each topic, or come up with additional facts for different topics. Tell students to supplement these facts by conducting research using a variety of available resources. Then have students write a short essay about one aspect of this topic. Encourage them to use at least five transitional words and phrases to help their writing flow.

American Civil War Facts

- 1861–1865

- Country is divided into the North and South

- Almost 200,000 African Americans fight with the Union Army

- Harriet Tubman helps in the Underground Railroad

- Battle of Gettysburg turns the tide of the war

- In 1863, Abraham Lincoln delivers the Emancipation Proclamation

Magna Carta Facts

- 1215

- English knights forced King John to sign

- King had to obey certain laws

- Raised taxes

- Trial by jury for people

- Beginning of democracy

Inclusion Tip

Post a list of transitional words on a bulletin board for students to use as a quick visual reference. Keeping wall charts allows kinesthetic or fidgety learners a constructive opportunity to get out of their seats during a writing assignment.

Make It Flow

Transitional words and phrases, or connecting words, help your writing flow from one thought to the next. Keep this list in a writing folder.

Addition

Again

Also

As well

Finally

First, Second, etc.

Further

Furthermore

In addition

In the first place, In the second place, etc.

Incidentally

Last

More important

Moreover

Next

Then

Contrast

Actually

At the same time

By contrast

Formerly

However

In any case

In contrast

In reality

In spite of this

Instead

Meanwhile

Nevertheless

On the contrary

On the other hand

Otherwise

Yet

Comparison

In like manner

In the same way

Likewise

Similarly

Whereas

Cause, Result, Purpose

Accordingly

As a result

Because of this

Consequently

For this reason

Hence

In this way

Knowing this

Of course

Then

To be specific

Therefore

Thus

With this in mind

Example, Restatement

For example

For instance

In brief

In conclusion

In fact

In particular

In other words

In short

More specifically

To summarize

Ultimately

At the same time

Before

During this time

Eventually

Finally

Frequently

In the future

In the meantime

Occasionally

Soon

Place

Behind

Beyond

Close by

Elsewhere

Further on

Here

In back

Nearby

On the left

On the opposite side

On the right

Opposite

There

Purposeful Writing

Completing numerous language arts exercises and worksheets may improve writing skills momentarily, but it does not teach students about purposeful writing. Writing letters, short stories, poems, editorials, and more, to pen pals, other students, friends, newspapers, and other audiences concretizes writing as a meaningful form of communication. This kind of writing connects students to larger issues and other people outside of their everyday experiences. Following are some purposeful writing ideas students can explore.

- Under your vigilant supervision, invite students to surf the net to find pen pals from around the world. This will certainly broaden students' horizons! Start with the following Web sites:

  - Surfing the Net with Kids:
    www.surfnetkids.com/penpals.htm

  - Friendship Through Education:
    www.friendshsiptrougheducation.org

- Contact local nursing homes and have students create a classroom "Adopt a Senior" program. Students could write letters to seniors who would appreciate the attentive communication. This communication definitely has two-way benefits!

- Have students write and share student-created picture books with younger students. This helps older students with organizational, research, interpersonal, and writing skills, while younger students are often more attentive to "teachers" closer to their own age.

- Create a classroom newspaper in which students write articles on current school and community events, sports, fashion, weather, local heroes, advice columns, movie and book reviews, and more. Share your newspaper with other classes.

- Encourage students to enter local poetry or short story writing contests. There are multitudes of contests and publishing opportunities for middle-school-age students:

  - Kids Bookshelf: www.Kidsbookshelf.com

  - Scholastic Art & Writing Awards: *www.scholastic.com/artandwritingawards/index.htm*

  - Amazing Kids' Amazing Writer's Library:
    www.amazing-kids.org/writers.htm#top

Speech Summaries

The purpose of this activity is to help students organize their ideas in a logical way. It also gives them the opportunity to process, disseminate, and evaluate given information.

Invite students to choose a speech from the list below, or find another one that interests them. You can find copies of these speeches in books or on the Internet. If possible, obtain CDs or audiotapes for students to listen to while they read the words, reinforcing both listening and reading skills.

Students can work cooperatively or independently to conduct research on these speeches using textbooks, encyclopedias, and online sources. Have them arrange the information into logical sentences, using the **Speech Summary reproducible (page 26)** as their guide. Invite students to add more sentences. Whether completing the task by themselves or with peers, everyone must rewrite the finished product, either by hand or on the computer.

Speech Choices

Patrick Henry's "Give Me Liberty, or Give Me Death" Speech (1775)

Washington's Farewell Address (1796)

Tecumseh's Speech to Governor William Harrison (1810)

The Gettysburg Address (1863)

Franklin Roosevelt's "Four Freedoms" Speech (1941)

John F. Kennedy's Inaugural Address (1961)

Martin Luther King Jr.'s "I Have a Dream" Speech (1963)

Ronald Reagan's "Challenger Space Shuttle Explosion" Speech (1986)

Inclusion Tip

Add visuals from corresponding time periods to assist concrete learners.

Speech Summary

Directions: After you have read or listened to the speech, complete this writing frame.

1st Paragraph (Introduction)

In the year _____, _____

gave a speech called _____.

This speech told about _____,

_____, and _____.

When the speech was given, it was a time of _____

_____.

2nd Paragraph (Add more details)

The tone of this speech was _____.

Many people were _____

when they heard this speech. Some significant points in the speech included

_____

_____, and

_____.

3rd Paragraph (Conclusion)

This speech is very important because _____

_____.

After it was delivered, _____

This speech is still remembered today because _____

To sum up, I believe that this speech teaches us _____

Newspaper Articles

Newspapers are wonderful educational tools. However, students with learning differences can be overwhelmed by newspapers, considering the amount of print and the often "high level" language used. This activity, **Read All About It! (page 28)**, breaks down a newspaper into comprehensible, less intimidating parts. Students will learn how all these parts make up the "whole" of the news.

Bring in newspapers for students to peruse. Place them in a box labeled *Here's What's Happening!* Add copies of easier-to-read periodicals, and print out acceptable online news articles as well.

Invite students to work in small groups to focus on one topic only, such as entertainment or international news. Point out that newspaper articles must answer the *who, what, when, where, why,* and *how* questions to provide all the important information.

Rotate weekly assignments of local, country, international, sports, and entertainment, so everyone has a chance to investigate each type of article. You may use this activity as a starting point for having students write their own school newspaper! Invite them to write about school events, sports, field trips, awards, and more.

Inclusion Tips

Invite students to write assignments on a calendar to keep track of articles for which they are responsible.

Writing Rubric

Students must realize that their writing has standards. The standards listed in the **Writing Rubric (page 29)** offer direct focus on writing elements, from introduction to sentence length, word choices, transitional words, grammar, spelling, and conclusion. This rubric can be used for self-review, peer review, or for one-on-one teacher/student conferences. This rubric is also a great student reference for various writing assignments to see where they are achieving and where they need improvement.

Name _____ Date _____

Read All About It!

Directions: Write facts about each topic, answering the questions: *Who? What? When? Where? Why?* and *How?* Write the source for where you found the information.

	Local (Neighborhood)	Country (United States)	International (Other Countries)	Sports	Entertainment (Movies, Music, Dance, TV)
Who?					
What?					
When?					
Where?					
Why?					
How?					
Source (Newspaper and Reporter):					

Reproducible

Name _____ Date _____

Writing Rubric

Directions: Use this writing rubric to score the writing.

Category	4–Excellent	3–Good	2–Fair	1–Needs Improvement
Introduction (Organization)	The introduction is inviting, states the main idea, and previews the rest of the paper.	The introduction clearly states the main idea and previews the rest of the paper, but is not inviting.	The introduction states the main idea, but does not adequately preview the rest of the paper or invite the reader to read on.	There is no clear introduction of the main idea or rest of the paper.
Transitions (Organization)	A variety of transitions are used and clearly show how ideas are connected.	Transitions clearly show how ideas are connected, but there is little variety.	Some transitions work well, but connections between other ideas are fuzzy.	Transitions between ideas are unclear or nonexistent.
Support for Topic (Content)	Relevant details give important information beyond the obvious or predictable.	Supporting details and information are relevant, but one key part is unsupported.	Supporting details and information are relevant, but several key parts are unsupported.	Supporting details and information are typically unclear or not related to the topic.
Focus on Topic (Content)	There is one clear, well-focused topic. The main idea is firmly supported by details.	The main idea is clear, but the supporting details are general.	The main idea is somewhat clear, but there is a need for more supporting details.	The main idea is not clear. There is a seemingly random collection of information.
Sentence Length (Sentence Fluency)	Every paragraph has sentences that vary in length.	Almost all paragraphs have sentences that vary in length.	Some sentences vary in length.	Sentences rarely vary in length.
Grammar and Spelling (Conventions)	There are no errors in grammar or spelling that distract the reader from the content.	One or two errors in grammar or spelling distract the reader from the content.	Three or four errors in grammar or spelling distract the reader from the content.	More than four errors in grammar or spelling distract the reader from the content.
Word Choice	Vivid words and phrases paint pictures in the reader's mind. The choice of words is accurate and natural.	Vivid words and phrases paint pictures in the reader's mind, but occasionally the words are used inaccurately.	Words used communicate clearly, but the writing lacks variety, punch, or flair.	Limited vocabulary does not communicate strongly or capture the reader's interest. Some words are overused and not very specific.
Conclusion (Organization)	The conclusion is strong and leaves the reader with a feeling of "getting it."	The conclusion is recognizable and ties up almost all the loose ends.	The conclusion is recognizable, but it does not tie up several loose ends.	There is no clear conclusion; the paper just ends.

Writing Planners

Help students realize that sketching their thoughts is not a waste of time, but yields a coherent, polished piece of writing. Whether they are informing, persuading, or describing, planning is essential! Writing planners help students organize their thoughts around a central topic. They allow students to sort through and select ideas before writing them down in a paragraph or essay.

Inclusion Tip

Include more visual prompts to help less abstract learners collect their thoughts. Most important, be aware of quieter or possibly depressed students who may be reaching out for recognition and responses to their written communication.

Personal Narrative Planner (page 31)

This personal narrative planner helps students organize their thoughts before writing. Remind students that narrative writing is often biographical. It can tell about an experience from their past, a recent or ongoing experience, or something that happened to someone else they know, such as a parent or grandparent. This particular planner invites students to focus on their own lives. Prompt students with questions that stimulate thinking. Ask: *What was your favorite memory? What is your life like now? What are your future plans?*

Sensory Writing Planner (page 32)

This planner helps students think of and add sensory elements to their writing. Students might begin by thinking of a place and then writing sensory words in the columns to describe that place. For example: *At the beach, I see colorful towels and umbrellas; I feel the hot sun on my skin; I smell the fresh ocean breeze; I hear crashing waves; I taste the salty ocean.* After completing the planner, have students write a paragraph.

Persuasive Writing Planner (page 33)

Students will use this planner to organize their ideas for persuasive essays. They can use the planner give reasons for and to support their argument. After they've filled in their planner, have them go back to revise their ideas, editing, deleting, adding, and reorganizing as necessary, before writing their essays.

Personal Narrative Planner

Directions: Write your thoughts about the past, present, and future in the boxes below. Write whatever comes to mind—words, phrases, or sentences.

Past: Remember some past events.

Present: Concentrate on now.

Future: Focus on thinking ahead.

Sensory Writing Planner

Directions: Use this planner to write sensory words for your essay or story.

See	Hear	Smell	Touch	Taste

Name _____ Date _____

Persuasive Writing Planner

Directions: Use this planner to help you write a persuasive essay. Make sure to give reasons and examples to support your argument.

1st Paragraph (Introduce the topic.)

(State your argument.) I think _____ .

(State first reason.) First, _____ .

(State second reason.) In addition, _____ .

(State third reason.) Also, _____ .

2nd Paragraph (Expand on first reason; give an example.)

3rd Paragraph (Expand on second reason; give an example.)

4th Paragraph (Expand on third reason; give an example.)

5th Paragraph (Sum up all three reasons; restate your argument.)

CHAPTER 3

Mathematics

Math is vital for developing critical thinking skills across the curriculum. Math is not just adding and subtracting; it also includes conceptual lessons such as estimating, visualizing, deducing, and recognizing patterns. Math helps students in everyday, real-life situations such as averaging test scores, shopping, making change, telling time, measuring, and much more.

Calculating Grades

Students may wonder how math skills apply to the "real world." Teaching purposeful, meaningful math in daily activities helps students see the benefits of math in their everyday lives. Next time you return a test grade, instead of writing the score, just write a fraction with the number of correct answers and the total amount of test problems. Ask students to then calculate their own grades. Calculators can be used to verify all answers.

Give students a copy of the **Making the Grade reproducible (page 35)**. They will use this sheet to calculate the grade of a fictional student. This helps students practice for calculating their own grades throughout the year. They can use the steps to determine their own grades across the curriculum, reinforcing math concepts of fractions, proportions, decimals, rounding, and percents. This sends a strong message that math is a valuable, everyday tool.

Inclusion Tip

If students are having difficulty with this procedure, determine which of the five steps requires more direct skill instruction, and conduct a small-group modeling lesson. Encourage students to continue self-monitoring their grades to become independent, reflective learners.

Making the Grade

Directions: Look at the scores in the chart. Then follow the steps to calculate the final grade this student received. Use this formula to calculate your own grades throughout the year.

1. Divide each numerator by its denominator to figure out the number grade. Remember to move the decimal two places to the right for a percent (%).
2. Find the sum total of all the grades.
3. Count the total number of grades.
4. Divide the grade total by that number to figure out the average.
5. Look at the Key to see what letter grade this student got on his report card.

Number Correct	Fraction Grade/ Percent (Step 1)	Average (Steps 2, 3, 4)	Grade (Step 5)
12 out of 15 correct	$\frac{12}{15} = 80\%$		
20 out of 25 correct			
30 out of 40 correct			
78 out of 80 correct			
17 out of 20 correct			

Key:
A = 90–100
B = 80–89
C = 70–79
D = 65–69
F = Below 65

Estimating Tips and Discounts

Estimating is a real-life math skill that applies to many situations. Some students may think a 20% off sale means they pay $20 less. When eating out, figuring the appropriate tip may be baffling, even for adults! These situations provide teachable and motivating ways to apply practical math to functional everyday activities. Invite students to practice these skills using the **Estimating Percentages reproducible (page 37)**.

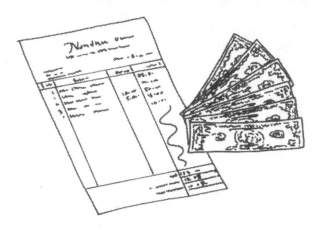

Inclusion Tip

Invite students to bring in store circulars with advertised discounts, and restaurant checks or menus to keep in a box labeled *Estimate It!* Encourage students to practice estimating tips and discounts during their free time.

Meaningful Connections

Meaningful connections help students view math beyond textbook pages. Like other math concepts, fractions, decimals, and percentages are easier to learn if they apply directly to students' lives.

Give students a copy of the **Fractions of My Day reproducible (page 38)**. This activity allows them to break down their day into individual activities and events. Students then figure out how much of their day they spend doing these activities and convert them to fractions and percentages. They might be surprised to find out how they really spend their time!

Inclusion Tip

Allow students to help each other check computations—fractions, decimals, and percentages—with a graphing calculator. Students with visual impairments or who could benefit from auditory cues can use talking calculators with headphones.

Estimating Percentages

Directions: Use this chart to guess, or estimate percentages. Then answer the questions below to calculate restaurant tips and store discounts.

Hint: Complete the 10% column first by moving the decimal one place to the left (i.e., $12.00 to $1.20). Then, to figure 5% simply divide that number in half (i.e., $1.20÷2 = $.60). For 50%, multiply 10% by 5 (i.e., $1.20 x 5 = $6.00). Some numbers are filled in to get you started.

Estimate Actual Amounts	5%	10%	15%	20%	25%	40%	50%	65%	70%
Actual: $11.75 Estimate: $12.00	$.60	$1.20							
Actual: $23.99 Estimate: $24.00									
Actual: $74.50 Estimate:									
Actual: $74.50 Estimate:									
Actual: $120.50 Estimate:									
Actual: $147.99 Estimate:									
Actual: $196.35 Estimate:									

Name _____ Date _____

Fractions of My Day

Directions: Figure out what fraction of your day you spend doing each of the following activities. Then convert those fractions to decimals and percents.

Activity	Fraction	Decimal	Percent
School			
Eating			
Sleeping			
TV			
Computer/Video			
Telephone			
Homework			
Reading			
Sports/Exercise			
Family			
Working/Chores			
Other Activities			
Totals:			
	No more than 24	No more than 1.00	No more than 100

Math Connections

Use the activities on pages 39–46 to actively involve students in a variety of math concepts. Students will calculate problems about themselves and their classmates, which helps focus their attention on the lesson. It also allows "fidgety" learners a structured opportunity to get out of their seats. It appeals to visual, kinesthetic, and auditory modalities.

The main thrust of these kinds of student-driven activities is that instead of doing repeated textbook problems, students internalize and apply the learning better when skills relate to their own personal experiences.

Inclusion Tip

Diversify prompts to include students' interests. Physical activities combined with personal connections equal retention.

Calculating Proportions and Ratios

Ask four students to stand in front of the class, while the class answers proportional questions such as:

- *What is the ratio of students wearing sneakers to those not wearing sneakers?*

- *What is the ratio of boys to girls, and then girls to boys?*

- *What is the ratio of students standing to those not standing, and then the ratio of those seated to those not seated?*

Calculating Rate

Ask students if they've ever been on a long car ride. Call on one student and use his or her response as a model for calculating rate (speed).

1. Ask the student where his or her family traveled and how long it took them to get there. For example, if the student knows the destination but isn't sure of the distance in miles, use a map with a scale of miles or find it on a computer mapping Web site.

2. Once the miles and time are known, introduce this formula to the class: $R = D/T$.

   Tell students that this is the formula for calculating rate, or speed (the average speed the car was traveling).

3. Before plugging in the known variables, have students write the definition for each letter in the formula:

   - $R = $ *Rate* or *Speed* (how fast the car was traveling)
   - $T = $ *Time*
   - $D = $ *Distance* (how far the car was traveling for each unit, or in this case, hour)

4. Plug in the variables and complete the calculation with students. Repeat using a variety of student-generated word problems.

Calculating Money

Ask students to name their favorite candy. If, for example, most students like jawbreakers, then ask them a question such as: *Would it be cheaper to buy a dozen jawbreakers for $1.50 or buy 12 at $0.15 each?*

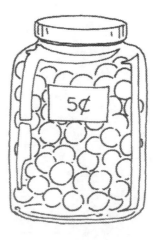

Living Equations

Algebra is a complex topic that can be simplified and introduced with concrete examples. In this activity, students physically demonstrate an algebraic equation, creating a 3-D visual the whole class can understand!

Example: 2x + 2 = 4

- Gather 11 students at the front of the class. Arrange them into a "living equation" by taping a piece of paper to the back of each student's shirt. Tape "x" on the first student, "+" on the second student, and "=" on the next student.

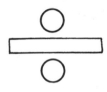

- Ask two students to stand before the "x" student, and two students to stand between the "+" student and the "=" student. Then ask four students to stand to the right of the "=" student.

- "Subtract" the two students from the left of the "equal" sign and two from the right of the "equal" sign. This concretely demonstrates that whatever you do to one side of an equation you must do to the other, like balancing a seesaw.

- Now students should see a human equation showing 2x = 2. There is no longer a need for the "+" sign, so have that student sit down.

- "Divide" each side of the equation by two so that "x" stands alone. This means that the left side loses its coefficient and remains "x," while the two students are divided into two groups of one each. Aha! Visual insight is now achieved, since x = 1.

- Substitute the answer into the original equation. Write it on the board: 2(1) + 2 = 4.

Inclusion Tips

Be sensitive to students who prefer or have to observe, but not physically participate in this lesson. Involve them by asking them to act as "algebraic scribes" and solve the equations.

To add more visuals, ask a student to record the lessons with a digital camera to create an algebra movie, casting students as variables, coefficients, and signs!

X Marks the Spot and Here's Y!

Variables can be a challenging concept for many students. Introduce and relate variables to money to offer students a valuable, concrete algebraic presentation.

Before complex equations can be solved, combine similar terms. Provide the following example for students:

Suppose you had just cleaned out your room and found 5 dollar bills, 6 quarters, 2 more dollar bills, and 3 more quarters. If you combine the dollar bills and the quarters, what numbers would complete this expression?

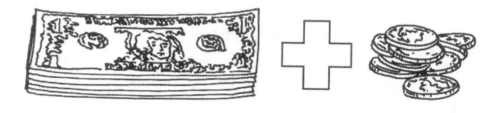

_____ dollar bills + _____ quarters

Now, let the x variable represent the number of dollar bills, and y represent the number of quarters. The expression representing dollar bills and quarters together is x + y.

The point here is that algebra is about letters meeting numbers, since different letters represent different values.

For equations using variables, always follow this simple rule: If there is a number in front of a letter, with no sign in between, then you multiply. For example, if $x = 3$, then $2x = 2 \times 3 = 6$.

After answering any questions students have about your presentation, distribute a copy of the **Various Variables reproducible (page 43)** to each student. Invite them to solve the equations using the variables shown.

Inclusion Tip

Concrete learners appreciate opportunities to see the abstract. Invite students to reflect on their learning by keeping a math journal. Use prompts such as: *I got it wrong because . . . I will use this when . . . This is easier now because . . . .*

Name _____ Date _____

Various Variables

Directions: Look at the equation chart below. Solve each equation based on the values of the variables shown (x and y).

1. $x = 5$ $y = 12$	$y - x =$	$2x + 2y =$	$x + 3 =$
2. $x = 3$ $y = 8$	$5y + 37 + 2y$	$8x + \frac{1}{2}y$	$3x + 2y + 2x - y$
3. $x = 10$ $y = 2.5$	$2x - 3y$	$y + y + y$	$5x + 10y$
4. $x = \frac{1}{3}$ $y = \frac{3}{4}$	$4x - y$	$\frac{1}{2}y + 2x$	$y \div x$

Now, suppose $x + y = 12$. Write some possible values of x and y.

$x =$ _____, _____, _____, _____, _____, _____, _____, _____, _____, _____

$y =$ _____, _____, _____, _____, _____, _____, _____, _____, _____, _____

Understanding Graphs

Students in the middle grades will have many opportunities to work with and plot graphs. Following are some simple strategies for helping students understand the concept of graphing. Make sure to use and explain all relevant graphing terms.

1. Demonstrate an x-axis and y-axis. Ask students to raise one hand high and place the other hand low to the ground to indicate the *y-axis*. Then have them stretch out both arms, one to the left and one to the right, to indicate the *x-axis*.

2. Further concretize this concept by relating the x-axis and y-axis to the names of local familiar street intersections. Reinforce the concepts by using the terms *vertical, horizontal,* and *perpendicular.*

3. Illustrate horizontal and vertical number lines for students that show both positive numbers and negative numbers.

4. Explain that the x-axis and y-axis are *perpendicular* to each other and form four regions. These regions, called *quadrants*, are labeled *I, II, III,* and *IV.* All points lay in these quadrants, unless one of their coordinates is directly on the x-axis or y-axis.

5. Distribute a copy of the **Graph It! reproducible (page 45)** to each student. Tell students to place their finger on the *origin* of the graph (0,0). Then, move across until they see a dot, either on the positive side (right) or negative side (left).

6. Direct students to look up and down where they stopped on the x-axis to locate the y coordinate. It can be located above the origin (positive number) or below the origin (negative number). Have students use what they learned to plot the graph.

Inclusion Tips

When establishing groups in any subject area, divide the class into *quadrants*, or sections, of the room. Ask students to write their names on the *x-axis*, or to line up like a *y-axis*. The objective is to apply math vocabulary across the curriculum.

Use geometer sketchpads to further concretize and demonstrate graphing concepts for visual and logical learners through technology.

Add tactile elements for sight-impaired students with manipulatives such as pipe cleaners, yarn, and string to separate and distinguish the quadrants, x-axis, and y-axis.

978-1-4129-5234-7

Graph It!

Directions: Identify these coordinates and quadrants. Then plot points I-P on the graph.

A. (0,3) Quadrants I and II

B. _____

C. _____

D. _____

E. _____

F. _____

G. _____

H. _____

I. (0,–3)

J. (–2,–2)

K. (5,4)

L. (1,–2)

M. (5,0)

N. (–4,–4)

O. (–5,4)

P. (4,3)

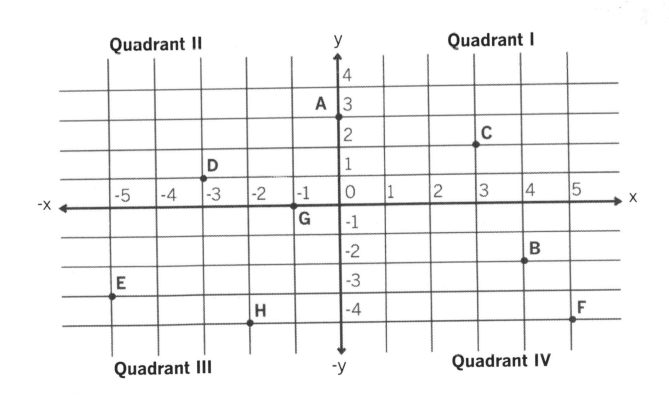

Creating and Understanding Tessellations

The value in creating tessellations is not just the finished product. The actual process involved can be a valuable learning tool. Students with learning differences often have difficulty with visual-motor integration. This activity helps students to connect visual-spatial elements with inferential reasoning to increase concentration and attention to detail. It is a lesson in both perseverance and geometric sense.

Tessellation Facts:

- Tessellations are designs, drawings, and/or patterns made with overlapping shapes of polygons.

- Tessellations date back to the Sumerian times in 4000 B.C.

- M. C. Escher, Bridget Riley, and Victor Vasarely are some famous artists whose work demonstrate tessellations.

Give students a copy of the **Terrific Tessellations reproducibles (page 47–49)**. Invite them to create and manipulate tessellations using the following materials:

- heavy construction paper marked with pencil in 3" x 3" grid squares

- index cards cut into 3" x 3" squares

- scissors

- erasers

- pencils

- glue

- tape

- crayons or markers

Tell students that even though the basic directions are the same, everyone's finished product will be different as they add their own colors and designs. To add a visual instructional element, invite students to watch a demonstration online at www.jimmcneill.com. Celebrate finished products by creating a classroom gallery!

Inclusion Tip

Students with learning differences often have perceptual impairments, including difficulties with spatial relationships, eye-hand coordination, directionality, and other visual tasks. Help these students by directly modeling each step, one at a time.

Terrific Tessellations: Translation

Directions: Follow these directions to make your own terrific tessellation designs!

1. Cut an index card into a 3 x 3 square. Draw a freeform line from the top left corner to the top right corner. See Figure A.

Figure A

2. Draw another freeform line from the top left corner to the bottom left corner. See Figure B.

Figure B

3. Cut out both shapes you drew, and save them for the next step.

Figure C

4. Move the top shape cutout to the bottom edge of the square, and tape it in place. See Figure C.

5. Move the left-side cutout to the right edge of the square, and tape it in place. This is your template. See Figure D.

Figure D

6. Place the new shape in the top left corner of your 3 x 3 paper grid sheet, lining up the corners with the grid square. Trace around your shape template. See Figure E.

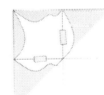

Figure E

7. Slide your shape to the next available grid square, line up the corners, and trace the template.

8. Continue sliding and tracing the template into any complete, open square until the grid sheet is full. Then erase the gridlines. See Figure F.

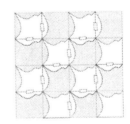

Figure F

9. Color in the negative space or draw repeated designs on the freeform shapes to make your own unique piece of artwork!

Terrific Tessellations: Rotation

Directions: Follow these directions to make your own terrific tessellation designs!

1. Repeat Steps 1 to 3 in Translations.

2. Move the top shape cutout to the right edge of the square, and tape it in place. See Figure G.

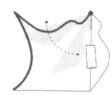

Figure G

3. Move the left-side cutout to the bottom edge of the square, and tape it in place. This is your template. See Figure H.

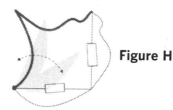

Figure H

4. Repeat Steps 6 to 9 in Translations, except each time you slide the shape to the next grid square, rotate it $\frac{1}{4}$ turn. See Figure I.

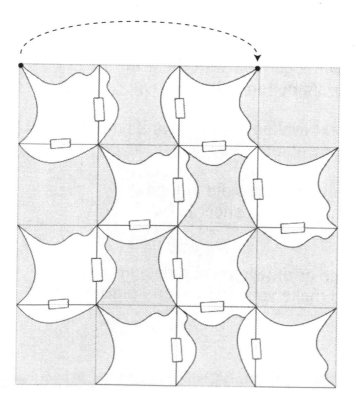

Figure I

Terrific Tessellations: Reflection

Directions: Follow these directions to make your own terrific tessellation designs!

1. Cut an index card into a 3 x 3 square. Draw a freeform line from the bottom left corner to the bottom right corner. See Figure J.

Figure J

2. Draw another freeform line from the bottom right corner to the top right corner. See Figure K.

Figure K

3. Cut out both shapes you drew, and save them for the next step.

4. Flip over both cutouts and place them on opposite sides of the square. Move the bottom cutout to the top of the square, and the right-side cutout to the left side of the square. Tape them in place. See Figure L.

Figure L

5. Place the new shape in the top left corner of your 3 x 3 paper grid sheet, lining up the corners with the grid square. Trace around your shape template.

6. Repeat Steps 6 to 9 in Translations, except each time you slide the shape to the next grid square, flip it over (not upside down, but as if you were turning a page in a book) to make the opposite shape. Hint: When you move to the next row, flip the template down. See Figure M.

Figure M

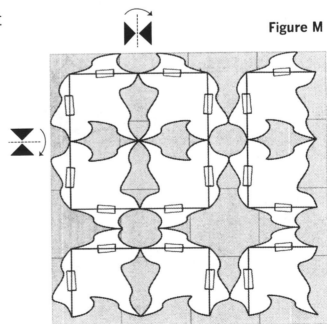

CHAPTER 4

Connecting Students to the Curriculum

Although specific standards must be achieved at each grade, teachers should first reach students on a level that they can understand and form relationships. Subjects such as math, science, reading, art, music, physical education, and social studies can be connected to each other and tied to students' lives in meaningful ways.

Teaching students how to relate to concepts across the curriculum plants seeds for important adult skills such as multi-tasking, thinking analytically, relating to varying situations, while applying learning to a multitude of events and situations. The lessons in this chapter try to engage intelligences across the curriculum. This is a time for growth in both academic and social situations.

Middle school students are often tempted by peers to conform and partake in situations that may not always be the wisest of choices. Direct skill instruction about peer pressure, proper nutrition, exercise, drugs, and alcohol is imperative for students in this age group, with both parents and teachers emphasizing healthy choices.

What Would Have Happened If . . . ?

This activity cannot be assessed using standardized tests, yet its value cannot be overemphasized. Nutrition, exercise, peer pressure, drugs, and alcohol are all valid issues that often affect students' academic

performance. Students sometimes experience an internal tug-of-war, struggling to make the right decisions. This activity provides teachers and parents the chance to listen, advise, and provide guidance.

Give students a copy of the **What Would Have Happened If . . . ? reproducible (page 52)**. These scenarios provide students with the opportunity to relate to particular situations and think about the consequences of unhealthy choices. At the same time, you purposefully address the curriculum through reading, writing, and discussion.

Inclusion Tip

If you discover a student is in a sensitive or dangerous situation, do not judge or embarrass him or her. Instead, contact a school guidance counselor, student study team members, a school nurse, parents, or administration, as appropriate. Immediately address all safety issues.

Television Talk Show

Whether we agree with it or not, television is part of students' lives. Inviting students to create their own television talk show is a fun, motivating exploration in research, writing, and presentation skills. This kind of student-guided learning activity proactively circumvents negative attention-seeking behavior and instead, focuses on student empowerment.

Give students a copy of the **Television Talk Show reproducible (page 53)**. Have them work in pairs to choose a person in each category to interview, and then come up with questions to ask each person. In order to ask relevant, interesting questions, students must research each person. This interdisciplinary lesson connects with many areas across the curriculum, while encouraging personal choice and cooperative learning.

Inclusion Tip

Invite students to switch roles so each has an opportunity to interview and be interviewed. Play to students' strengths and preferences, as some students will perform better and enjoy playing a particular role.

What Would Have Happened If . . . ?

Part 1: Pair up with a classmate or classroom volunteer. Choose one of the people below, and "plug in" the information to complete this sentence: *What would have happened if . . . ?*

Then, with your partner, write a short paragraph that expands on one idea. Be prepared to share your ideas with the class.

1. George Washington didn't eat healthy foods and had no energy to cross the Delaware?

2. Martin Luther King, Jr. had decided that civil rights weren't worth the fight?

3. Michelangelo spent his time drinking alcohol instead of painting?

4. Lance Armstrong didn't exercise properly before the bike race?

5. Christopher Reeve had given up the hope of walking?

6. Helen Keller's parents and teacher assumed she could never learn?

7. Jackie Robinson played video games all day instead of practicing baseball?

8. Marie Curie was not allowed to research radium because she was a woman?

Part 2: Now, complete the sentence for both you and your partner. Here are some examples:

1. What if I decided not to finish school?

2. What if I didn't try very hard to make the soccer team?

3. What if I only ate potato chips and ice cream?

4. What if I stayed up late and only got three hours of sleep a night?

5. What if I decided to start smoking because my friend pressured me?

Name _____   Date _____

Television Talk Show

Directions: Congratulations! Television executives have decided that you have what it takes to host your own talk show. You can choose whom to interview for each of the following categories. The best part is that your guests have the ability to travel through time, so they can be living or from the past. Think of two questions you'd like to ask each guest and write it in the chart.

Category	Person's Name	Question 1	Question 2
Actor/Actress			
Musician/Singer			
Artist			
Author			
Scientist			
Politician			
Explorer			
Inventor			
Athlete			
Nobel Prize Winner			

Now, work with a partner to role-play an interview with one of these interesting people! Present your role play to the class.

Different Ways of Learning

Saying that students learn differently within the "multiple intelligences" is really just another way of saying that each student is unique! Self-awareness of likes and dislikes is important for learners of all ages. You should also be aware of your own preferred (stronger) and weaker intelligences. If you do not like a subject, you might subliminally send out negative messages to students, such as *I don't like or feel comfortable with this topic.* All intelligences and students have value!

Give students a copy of the **Different Ways of Learning reproducible (page 55)**. Invite them to look at the pictures and think about which activities they like best and least. Help students rank the activities by writing the numbers 1–8 in the boxes.

The multiple intelligences are labeled as follows:

- Verbal/Linguistic—Book Smart

- Interpersonal—People Smart

- Bodily-Kinesthetic—Body Smart

- Visual/Spatial—Picture Smart

- Logical/Mathematical—Number Smart

- Naturalistic—Nature Smart

- Intrapersonal—Self Smart

- Musical Rhythmic—Music Smart

- Existential—Question/Philosophy Smart (Beyond What You See)

Inclusion Tip

Place students in groups according to their favorite activities, and ask them to discuss their preferences. Then place students in groups according to their least favorite activities. Encourage them to discuss whether they dislike certain activities or just feel they are not talented in these areas. Post "intelligences" signs around the room as reminders that it's okay to learn in different ways!

978-1-4129-5234-7

Different Ways of Learning

Directions: Look at the pictures in the boxes. Label all the boxes, from 1 to 9. Write 1 in the box that shows what you like to do best. Number your least favorite activity 9.

Book Smart Reading and writing	People Smart Working in groups and being with friends	Body Smart Dancing and sports
_____ 	_____ 	_____ 
Picture Smart Putting pictures together	Self Smart Thinking and being by myself	Number Smart Math and computers
_____ 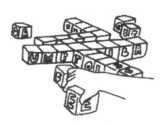	_____ 	_____ 
Nature Smart Being in nature	Music Smart Singing and playing musical instruments	Question Smart Exploring questions and answers
_____ 	_____ 	_____ 

Student Teachers

There is no better way to learn something than to teach it to others! Let students in on some of your teaching strategies by allowing them to help you teach some class lessons. Relinquishing power to students is actually freeing you to better monitor and help students without singling out learners who are more sensitive to classmates' opinions.

Pair up each student with a partner. Tell students that they will be teaching one topic from each subject area to the class. Provide each pair with a copy of the **You Are the Teacher! reproducible (page 57)**. Have student pairs choose a topic from each of the following subjects: social studies, math, science, art/music, writing, or reading.

Once students have chosen topics, assign presentation dates. You may choose to have monthly or quarterly presentations, with different pairs presenting on assigned days each week. Most likely, students will find new respect for the time you devote to lesson planning!

To help students get started with lesson plans, discuss the following questions as a class:

Anaconda

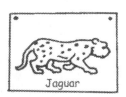

Jaguar

Toucan

- How will you teach the topic to the rest of the class?

- What materials will you need for the lesson?

- Will you lecture and/or have students complete work together or independently?

- Will you have visuals such as a PowerPoint presentation, digital storytelling, worksheets, or overheads?

- What important facts/details do you want students to learn?

- Can you create a game for the other students to play that will help them to learn more about the topic?

- How will you and your partner co-teach the lesson?

- What quiz or test will you give students to find out if the lesson was successful?

- What homework will you assign?

Inclusion Tip

Allow students to present their lesson in any way that makes them comfortable, such as using a slide or PowerPoint presentation, music, classroom guests, or interactive activities.

978-1-4129-5234-7

Name _____ Date _____

You Are the Teacher!

Directions: Choose a topic from each subject to teach to the class.

Social Studies	Math	Science	Art/Music	Language Arts
World geography	Division	Recycling	Abstract painting	Capitalization
World War II	Probability	Human life	Watercolor painting	Verb tenses
Civil War	Algebraic equations	Astronomy	Perspective	Business letters
American Revolution	Graphs	Chemistry	Sketching still life	Literary elements
Economics	Solving word problems	Plants/Rain forest	Impressionism	Transitions
Political	Tessellations	Physics	Rhythm	Poetic terms
Citizenship	Geometry	Oceans	Classical music	Sequencing events
Imperialism	Patterns	Food chain	Reading music	Figurative language
World cultures	Estimations	Geology	Famous composers	Editing/ proofreading
Renaissance	Ratios	Genetics	World music	Identifying the main idea

CHAPTER 5

Comprehension and Study Skills

The time students spend in school is only the beginning of where learning takes place. Educators will acknowledge that the students who do best in class are those who also complete homework assignments on time and review learned concepts at home. It's important to instill these good study habits, while encouraging the home-to-school connection.

The purpose of the following reproducibles is to increase student awareness of how efforts at home and school have positive consequences. Students will realize that successful learning output does not occur spontaneously, but is related to their efforts.

When teaching in an inclusive classroom, many questions need to be considered.

- How are the facts delivered?

- Do lessons incorporate technology?

- Are students active participants in their learning?

- Are students' strengths honored and embraced?

- Are charts or graphic organizers available?

- Do students have well-organized, legible notes to study?

- Are the lessons' concepts presented in a step-by-step fashion that ascertains prior knowledge before learning assumptions are made?

- Are there ample visuals?

- Are there opportunities for cooperative learning experiences?

- Are ideas and concepts revisited before formal assessment?

There are many questions, with no simple answers! The following activities address many of these issues, offering students a variety of ways to study and evaluate what they know. Students with lower cognitive levels or attention/disorganization issues benefit greatly from these types of activities.

Concept Map (page 60)

Organization of information often determines how much students remember. This concept map allows students to pack a lot of details and information into a concise study guide.

Self-Determination (page 61)

These principles encourage students to reflect on their "learning attitudes." A positive attitude can often open up students' minds to learning and accepting information.

Thinking About Learning (page 62)

Some students excel in certain topics, while others struggle. This reproducible allows students to evaluate their level of proficiency in any given topic, and guides them in finding ways to improve.

Study Skills Checklist (page 63)

This comprehensive checklist provides students with multitudes of strategies for studying. Tell students to keep this sheet as a study reference throughout the year.

Following Directions (page 64)

Mastering both oral and written instructions is crucial to doing well on standardized tests, including always carefully reading directions and questions. This activity provides a lesson students will not soon forget!

Mnemonic Devices (page 65)

Mnemonic devices are valuable memory tools that help students who experience concept overload. When there's an array of concepts on an assessment, students with lower cognitive skills and learning differences may become frustrated if they can't remember it all. Mnemonic devices can help!

Studying PAYs Off! (page 66)

This activity reminds students that learning is not just a regurgitation of facts but also processing and synthesizing information. Using the PAY method, students will learn to guide themselves to better learning habits.

Concept Map

Directions: Use this concept map to organize information about specific topics. Remember to just list key words and phrases.

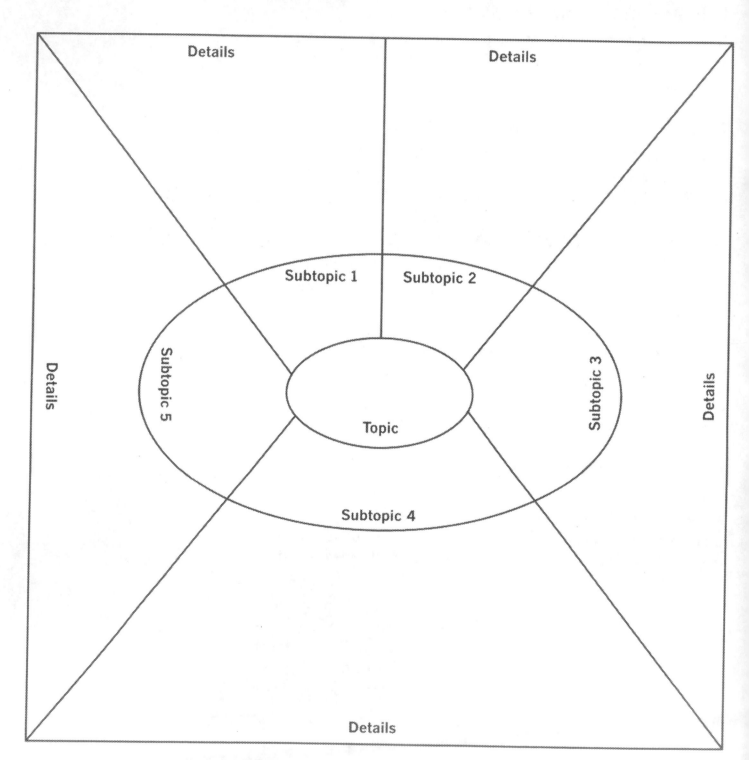

Name _____ Date _____

Self-Determination

Directions: Read each principle of self-determination below. Then circle one sentence in each column that describes you best. If you have any other comments or thoughts, write them on the back of this paper.

Principles of Self-Determination	Academic Situations	Social Situations
Know yourself	"I guess I got it," OR "I really do not understand this stuff!"	"I don't have a lot of friends." OR "The whole class is mean."
Value yourself	"Maybe I can figure it out another way." OR "I'll never get it!"	"I think I am a good person." OR "There's something wrong with me."
Plan	"I'll review it when I get home, or maybe I can ask the teacher or a friend for help." OR "Who has time for this? It's just not important!"	"I need to talk to the guidance counselor about this." OR "Who cares? That's just the way it is!"
Act	"Could you please explain that again, or what else can I do to understand this?" OR "Maybe I'll get lucky on the test!"	"The counselor gave me really good advice on how to act with other kids." OR "I'll just stick to myself."
Experience outcomes	"I'm sure glad I got some additional help!" OR "I can't believe I failed!	"I'm glad I'm not alone at lunchtime anymore." OR "Those kids are mean for leaving me out."
Learn	"Next time, I'll ask for help when I don't understand something." OR "That test was unfair!"	"I'll remember how my positive attitude affects how other kids treat me." OR "I can't understand why nothing changes."

Thinking About Learning

Directions: Rate the difficulty level of an assignment. Be honest with yourself as you evaluate your understanding of the topic. If you find that you are not sure or are very confused about a topic, ask a teacher, peer, or teacher's assistant for help. This will keep you on the right track!

Name: _____ Date: _____

Subject: _____

Topic: _____

Text Pages and/or Assignment: _____

Circle the rating: E, M or T.

  E = Easy "I understand this!

  M = Medium "I'm not sure about this topic."

  T = Tough "Hard to understand."

My comments: _____

_____

_____

_____

_____

_____

_____

_____

_____

Name _____ Date _____

Study Skills Checklist

Directions: Check off all the ways you can improve your study skills!

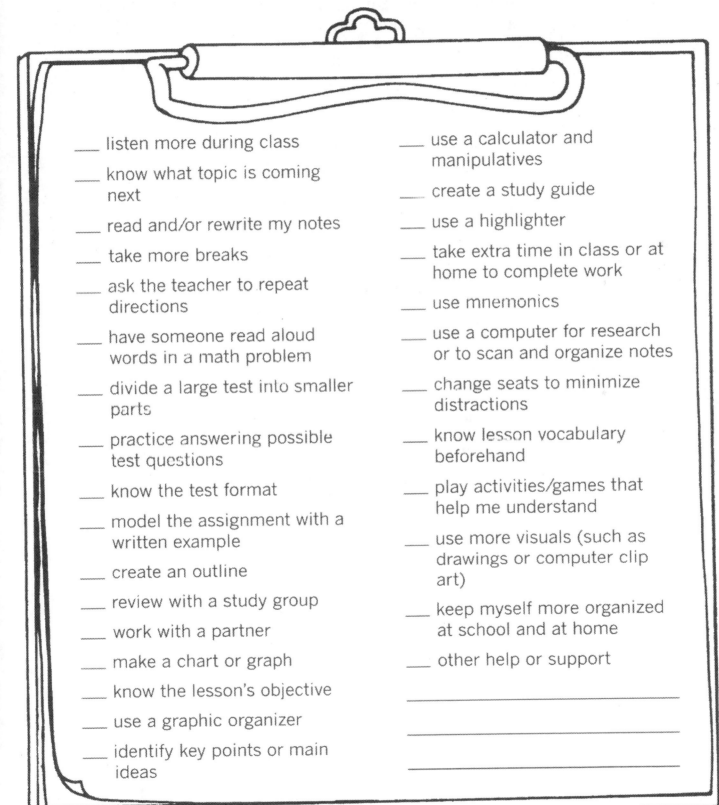

____ listen more during class

____ know what topic is coming next

____ read and/or rewrite my notes

____ take more breaks

____ ask the teacher to repeat directions

____ have someone read aloud words in a math problem

____ divide a large test into smaller parts

____ practice answering possible test questions

____ know the test format

____ model the assignment with a written example

____ create an outline

____ review with a study group

____ work with a partner

____ make a chart or graph

____ know the lesson's objective

____ use a graphic organizer

____ identify key points or main ideas

____ use a calculator and manipulatives

____ create a study guide

____ use a highlighter

____ take extra time in class or at home to complete work

____ use mnemonics

____ use a computer for research or to scan and organize notes

____ change seats to minimize distractions

____ know lesson vocabulary beforehand

____ play activities/games that help me understand

____ use more visuals (such as drawings or computer clip art)

____ keep myself more organized at school and at home

____ other help or support

_____

_____

_____

Following Directions

Directions: This is a five-minute, timed exercise on different school topics. Read all the questions before you begin.

1. Write your name and the date at the top of the page.

2. Underline the word *exercise*.

3. Write the odd numbers from *1* to *49*.

4. List the seven continents in alphabetical order.

5. Write the lowercase alphabet in cursive or manuscript.

6. Draw a picture of something that is recyclable.

7. Write the title of your favorite book.

8. List five words that rhyme with *school*.

9. Write, "I love school!" twenty times.

10. Now that you have read everything, do numbers 1 and 2 only, and then patiently wait and watch classmates complete the worksheet.

The lesson: Always read directions very carefully!

Mnemonic Devices

Mnemonics are words or short phrases that help you recall facts, rules, concepts, or information. Mnemonics are valuable study tools.

This mnemonic device will help you pay attention in class: **Watch Me Focus With Interest!**

Watch = words

Me = meaning

Focus = focus

With = write notes and wait to ask questions

Interest = be interested

1. Concentrate on **W**ords being said in class, without predicting or connecting everything to your own life. Otherwise you might miss the lesson.

2. Listen to the actual words, but think about the **M**eaning of those words.

3. **F**ocus on your teacher or the person speaking. Don't be distracted by other things, such as other students talking or looking out the window. Pay close attention!

4. **W**rite notes on important facts or items you are unsure about, but **W**ait to ask questions. Your teacher may answer them during the lesson!

5. Be **I**nterested in what you are learning, even if you think it is boring!

   Other common mnemonic devices include Roy G. Biv (colors of the rainbow: Red, Orange, Yellow, Green, Blue, Indigo, Violet) and My Very Educated Mother Just Served Us Nuts (eight planets in our solar system, in order from the sun: Mercury, Venus, Earth, Mars, Jupiter, Saturn, Uranus, Neptune).

   Create your own mnemonic devices to help you study.

Name _____ Date _____

Studying PAYs Off!

Use the PAY method to help you study lessons or new concepts.

Paraphrase	**A**greement	**Y**our Action
1. Read the text and/or class notes from the lesson.	1. Form your own opinion about what you heard in class, read in textbooks, or researched online.	1. Will this information affect you in any way?
2. Think about the information.	2. Explain whether you think this information is important or unimportant.	2. What actions will you take now, based upon this information?
3. Write about what you read and/or heard, in your own words, summarizing the main points. You can use all computer tools (e.g., language, grammar, and spell checks) to correct written work.	3. Do you agree with these facts? Why or why not?	3. Have these facts in any way altered or changed your life or thinking?

CHAPTER 6

Reflective Assessment, Testing, and Grading

Before considering alternate assessments, look carefully at the general education curriculum requirements. In the past, learners with special needs were often removed from "mainstream" learning and placed in separate classes with lower requirements. Unfortunately, this resulted with many adults being ill prepared to meet societal demands.

Assessments take many shapes and forms. Grades can be obtained from portfolios, observations, paper or oral tests and quizzes, homework, reports, class projects, class participation, and more. Students with special needs often do not fare well with typical assessments. Reasons for failure can vary from lower cognitive levels, poor or inappropriate instruction, and sometimes a lack of motivation and/or attention.

This situation calls for both you and the student to challenge your way of thinking. Ask yourself: *Is there another way I can teach this subject to* this student? Students should ask themselves: *Have I tried my best?* Both teachers and students should be involved in the assessment process.

The activities in this section vary from typical assessments to those with formats that correspond with the multiple intelligences and individual differences. Students will reflect on whether they have memorized concepts, or in fact, actually retained them for long-term learning. These sample assessments are content specific, yet their format can be applied to many subjects

Create Your Own Test

With this activity, the test is the test! Almost nothing is a better assessment for understanding a subject than to write a test for it. This activity integrates a variety of skills, including reading, writing, math, critical thinking, and synthesizing and breaking down information.

Give students a copy of the **Create Your Own Test reproducible (page 69)**. Ask them to work in pairs or small, cooperative groups to review subjects and create a test based on the main concepts. The final product will reveal learned concepts as well as areas for improvement. Encourage students to include a variety of test questions, including multiple choice, true/false, matching, essay, short answer, and long answer. Provide a sample of each type of question. Make sure students include an answer key with their test.

Later, you can choose one of the student-created tests to give as an actual assessment. Or, you can have student groups exchange tests with each other to "grade" each other's work as well as evaluate their own learning about the subject.

Inclusion Tip

As you circulate around the classroom assisting students, look out for individual behavioral and academic needs. This is a great time for mini-lessons on topics such as dividing responsibilities for cooperative work or correcting sentence structure. Take advantage of these teachable moments!

Create Your Own Test

Directions: Write a test based on your texts, class notes, and research. Use the following question starters to help you. Follow these directions for writing your test:

- Vary the types of questions. Write *short* and *long answer* questions. A *short answer* question can be answered with one or two words. A *long answer* question requires an explanation or description.
- Vary your questions by including:

  True/False   Multiple choice

  Essay   Matching
- Create an answer key by writing the answers on a separate sheet of paper.
- Decide the score (points given for a correct answer) for each question. The total test score should add up to 100.

Sample Questions:

Short answer question: *What is the story's setting?*
Long answer question: *Why do you think the main character changed her mind?*

Test Questions:

1. What is _____?

2. Where is _____?

3. How is _____?

4. How did _____?

5. Why did _____?

6. When did _____?

7. Which is not an example of _____?

8. Tell the difference between _____ and _____ .

9. _____

10. _____

Subject/Genre Board Games

Board games can be both a reflection on learning and an assessment of students' knowledge. This activity allows students to display reading, writing, math, research, organizational, and interpersonal skills. It's an excellent review, offers opportunities for further exploration, and serves as an assessment to demonstrate understanding.

Have students work in small groups to choose a game, subject, and genre around which to design their games. For example, copy the game *Trouble*. The subject is *American history,* and the genre is *autobiography.* In this example, create game cards on which Abraham Lincoln asks riddles about where and how he grew up, his presidency, the Civil War, the Emancipation Proclamation, and how he was assassinated,

To create their games, students will need to create:

- Rules for how to play, with step-by-step directions

- Playing pieces or characters

- Board layout

- Box for the game

- Drawings or clip art

- Information (facts and notes) about the subject

- Other materials (e.g., play money, sound effects)

Provide students with the following list of subjects, games, and genres. Ask them to choose from this list or come up with their own ideas.

Subjects	Games to Imitate	Genres
Math	Candy Land®	Fairy Tale
Science	Scrabble®	Science Fiction
Social Studies	Monopoly®	Biography
Reading/Writing	Trouble®	Autobiography
World Cultures	Life®	Historical Fiction
Art	Checkers	Mystery
Physical Education	Chess	Nonfiction
Music	Chutes and Ladders®	Fiction
Computers	Wheel of Fortune®	Poem
Health	Jeopardy®	Newspaper

978-1-4129-5234-7

Vivid Visuals

This is an example of an assessment format that includes visuals, rather than just text. Students who need pictures and other visual concepts to solidify learning benefit from this kind of assessment. This is just one example of how to use visuals to assess student learning.

Give students a copy of the **Who Are They? reproducible (page 72)**. Have them examine the visual associated with each person. The objective of this activity is for students to identify historical figures, find and list a couple of facts about each one, categorize them, and then order them on a timeline. This kind of assessment is effective across the curriculum to identify, categorize, and relate concepts.

Inclusion Tip

Since many students are visual learners, try to include pictures with both instruction and assessment. If text does not have visuals, ask students who like to draw to pair up with a partner to illustrate or find clip art that correlates with the concepts.

Economical Words

Sometimes when students select correct answers on matching or multiple-choice assessments, they have little knowledge of what the words actually mean. This is called "rote studying" or "learning for the test." This sample assessment, **Economical Words (page 73)**, is not about memorization, but linking words and definitions with conceptual understanding.

The objective is to offer students a structured open-book test that allows them to connect word meaning with both definitions and context. This interdisciplinary strategy also connects assessment with purposeful writing. Writing itself can be the assessment across many subject areas, without being exclusive to language arts.

Inclusion Tip

Structure is essential for students who require external organization. Students with communication and language difficulties do better when they can see categories first and then respond to the information.

Who Are They!

Directions: Find two interesting facts about each person. Then group the people in categories such as politics, civil rights, science, music, and so on. Finally, sequence them on a historical timeline.

Jackie Robinson	Julius Caesar	Leonardo da Vinci	Marie Curie
Wolfgang Amadeus Mozart	Susan B. Anthony	Abraham Lincoln	Harriet Tubman
Albert Einstein $E = mc^2$	George Washington	Benjamin Franklin	Galileo

Economical Words

Directions: Write a definition or synonym for each
economics word. Choose any ten of these words and write
a paragraph that demonstrates your understanding of the vocabulary.
Use a separate sheet of paper for your paragraph.

Economics Words	Definitions (Synonyms)
want	would like, desire
need	can't do without, require
buyer	
seller	
barter	
supply	
demand	
goods	
services	
price	
consumer	
economy	
labor	
business	
incentive	
monopoly	
capital	
taxes	

Review What You Learned

Not all assessments should be "formal" in a diverse classroom. Open-ended assessments allow students to really show what they've learned instead of simply choosing, or even guessing names, dates, and random facts on a standard test.

The graphic organizer **Review What You Learned (page 75)** provides a simple, open-ended way for students to describe major points or concepts learned in any of the content areas. Using this type of assessment routinely in your classroom should decrease student apathy and inspire them to ask more questions and prepare more comprehensively for tests. Use this sheet over and over again for assessments across the curriculum.

Inclusion Tip

Inform students of the grading system you are using. In this case, you might score each complete and accurate response at 10 points, with partial credit given for incomplete responses. If possible, model samples of poor, fair, good, and excellent answers so expectations are clear.

Student Self-Assessment

Why should teachers be the only ones allowed to give grades? Self-grading is an effective way for students to truly evaluate their academic performance and effort put forth in class and at home. **My Report Card (page 76)** is an in-depth version of a K-W-L chart. This form asks students to reflect on what they know about a subject, what they learned about the subject, and what they would like to learn more about in the future. Students must then grade themselves and explain why they chose this grade.

Meet with students individually to review their Self-Assessment Forms. Praise successes and strides, and guide students to see where they need improvement.

Inclusion Tip

Use this assessment as an opportunity to increase communication with students who sometimes get lost in the "shuffle" and need more self-confidence and recognition. Encourage students with lower self-esteem to give themselves credit for their efforts and progress, even though they may not have mastered all concepts.

Name _____ Date _____

Review What You Learned

Directions: Describe five important things you learned about the topic.

Topic: _____

1. _____
_____
_____

2. _____
_____
_____

3. _____
_____
_____

4. _____
_____
_____

5. _____
_____
_____

My Report Card

Directions: Complete the following statements to reflect on your learning.

MATH		A
SCIENCE		C
LANGUAGE		A
SOCIAL STUDIES		B
P.E.		B

Before I learned about _____

I thought _____

_____

Now I know _____

_____

This subject/topic/concept relates to _____

_____

I would like to research more information about _____

_____

I would like to research more information about _____

If I were going to grade myself on what I've learned, I would give myself a _____

I would give myself this grade because _____

_____

_____

My report card comments would include _____

_____

_____

Reproducible   978-1-4129-5234-7 • © Corwin Press

CHAPTER 7

Creating a Climate for Classroom Acceptance

Even if you have minimal experience instructing students with exceptionalities, you can still achieve successful inclusion for all students! First, establish a level of comfort and trust amongst you, the students, and their parents. Second, increase your knowledge of cognitive, behavioral, sensory, communication, physical, and learning differences. Most important, maintain a positive mindset, which most often yields positive and beneficial inclusion results.

Accepting others should come naturally to all of us. However, in some cases, people with exceptionalities or differences are often the recipients of negative and unfounded perceptions and prejudices. In today's inclusive classrooms, students need help realizing that there are differences amongst all of us. Through early training, students can learn to accept people as they really are and maximize the potential of who they can be. A positive classroom climate will create an atmosphere of acceptance where all individuals are valued!

Model appropriate inclusive etiquette and encourage students to role-play possible classroom scenarios to maximize not only academic, but also social opportunities for acceptance. The activities on pages 78–83 act as conduits to merit abilities, encourage reflections, and promote positive peer interactions. Walk through each activity with students, encouraging them to share their thoughts and feelings along the way. Students will realize that everyone has strengths and weaknesses. Remember to focus on their strengths!

Middle school students often try to establish their place in the classroom and school, with peers conforming to the norm. These activities shake that thought by reestablishing the definition of "normal" and allowing students to draw conclusions through discussion, simulations, associations, and reflections.

Inclusion Tip

Invite guest speakers with disabilities to talk with students about their successes and struggles. Encourage an open question-answer forum designed to confront misconceptions and dissolve biases.

Perception vs. Reality

Confusion between the left and right sides of the brain can sometimes make simple activities seem difficult. For example, the right part of the brain might recognize a shape, but the left side of the brain wants to read the name of that shape, even if it's incorrect.

To reinforce this concept, draw several shapes on the board, and write the incorrect names inside the shapes. Ask student volunteers to tell you what they see. Accept varied responses and self-corrections. Then discuss possible misperception and misinterpretation. This activity reminds students that their perceptions can interfere with learning.

Explain to students that some people face these types of difficulties every day. They might not always see or understand things as others do. Students with learning challenges must deal with a variety of issues—social, cognitive, academic, and/or physical.

Inclusion Tip

Share your own personal frustrations when your perceptions or skills were different than others' (e.g., first time attending a dance class, playing a new musical instrument, or trying to communicate in a foreign country when you did not know the language).

What Do You See?

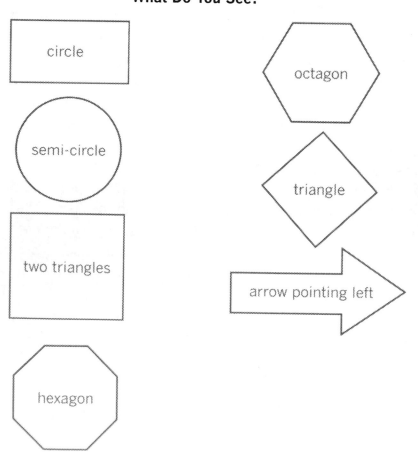

Something to Think About

This is a great introductory activity to get students thinking about how people with differences and exceptionalities can succeed in life. Read each statement to students, and ask them to tell you if it is true or false. Lead a class discussion about the ABILITIES of all people.

- A person with one arm can be a physical therapist.

- A person with Down Syndrome can be successful in school.

- A person who is blind can "read" a visual dictionary.

- A person with dyslexia can go to college.

- People with cerebral palsy can be public speakers.

- A person with autism can find and keep a good job.

- An artist without hands can create beautiful art.

- A person with cognitive impairments can have children of his or her own.

- A person who is blind can run in a marathon.

- A person who is deaf can be a college professor.

- People with disabilities need opportunities to show their abilities.

Now, write the word *disABILITY* on the board. Ask students the following questions, and initiate whole-group discussion.

- Why is the base word of *disABILITY* capitalized and underlined in this sentence?

- Do you know someone with a *disABILITY*, or someone who learns or does things different than most people?

- Have you ever heard of someone with a *disABILITY* being treated unfairly?

- If you had a *disABILITY*, how would you want others to treat you?

A Helping Hand

Directions: Think carefully about each question below. With a partner, write about how you could help each of these students.

How would you help a student who . . .

1. . . . needed more attention from the teacher?

2. . . . wanted lessons repeated a lot?

3. . . . could not read the same book as you and your classmates?

4. . . . required more time to complete assignments?

5. . . . could not see well or was sight impaired?

6. . . . had very sloppy handwriting?

7. . . . could not hear some sounds or was hearing impaired?

8. . . . had trouble sitting quietly?

9. . . . required more time to complete tests?

10. . . . tried his or her best, but kept failing tests?

11. . . . did less homework than everyone else?

12. . . . was unable to take notes like the rest of the class?

What Is "Normal"?

Directions: Write what you think is "normal" and "weird" for each of the following topics.

1. Normal food _____

Weird food _____

2. Normal clothes _____

Weird clothes _____

3. Normal book _____

Weird book _____

4. Normal movie _____

Weird movie _____

5. Normal music _____

Weird music _____

6. Normal hobby _____

Weird hobby _____

7. Normal student? _____

Things to think and talk about:

- Why does everyone have different answers?
- Can the word *normal* really be defined?

The Chemistry of Friendship

Chemistry is the science of matter, the branch of the natural sciences dealing with the composition of substances and their properties and reactions.

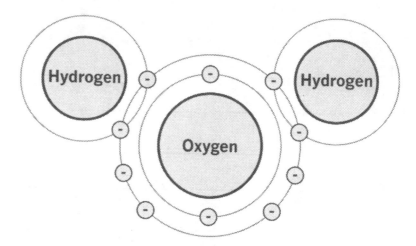

Two hydrogen atoms interact with an oxygen atom to create a water molecule.

There are many elements in the periodic table, just as there are in the classroom. Elements in the periodic table are arranged according to their properties. Introduce to students the properties of several elements in this table, such as water. For example, water can be a liquid, a gas, or a solid.

Create an analogy for students, comparing elements' different properties to people's different abilities. Invite students to think of friends or other people they know who have different "properties," or abilities. Just as elements interact differently, so do people!

In a brief paragraph, ask students to describe the chemistry of reactions between students in your classroom. Are some student reactions better than others, with good bonding, or are some more explosive? Have students describe the chemistry in your classroom, focusing on everyone's abilities! Invite volunteers to share their work with the class to initiate class discussion.

Inclusion Tip

If this chemistry analogy is too difficult for some students, ask them to think about other combinations, such as mixing together primary colors to create secondary ones, putting different members of a rock band together to perform a song, or combining different ingredients together to make cookie batter.

978-1-4129-5234-7

Disability Awareness Rubric (for Teachers and Staff)

Read each row across, and then circle the statement in the first, second, or third column that best describes you. Total your points below to find your "disability awareness" score.

Lower Expectations (1 point each)	Minimal Expectations (2 points each)	Exceed Expectations (3 points each)
Think students with disabilities are not really as capable as students without disabilities	Think students with disabilities can have limited achievements, but are still not comparable to students without disabilities	Think students with disabilities are just as capable or may have even more competencies than peers without disabilities
• Focus on the students' weaknesses • Think difficulties will hinder classroom progress with academics and peers	Aware of students' weaknesses, but think students can achieve a few academic and social strides	• Concentrate on students as individuals, looking beyond the disabilities toward student strengths • Teach the students compensatory strategies to achieve school successes
• Automatically delete more difficult assignments for classified students • Think they will never achieve the same learning objectives as other students	Allow students with disabilities to try some activities, but have lower expectations	Exhibit high expectations for all students, establishing prior knowledge to determine instructional levels
See students' disabilities in the foreground, without recognizing that it is just one part of an individual's makeup	Know that students with disabilities have individual personalities, but think the disability is the primary focus	Teach and communicate with individual students, using language and behaviors that focus on the student, not the disability
• Think students with disabilities will not achieve levels of independence and need only functional skills in school settings • Think their instruction interferes with the learning needs of other students	Want to help students with disabilities, but think classroom modifications can actually harm and enable, thereby not guiding students toward an adult level of independence	Believe students with disabilities will lead productive, independent lives as members of the community when given the proper accommodations, supports, and training in school settings
Believe students with disabilities should be educated in separate settings with different curriculums than peers without disabilities	Think some students with disabilities can be mainstreamed into regular classes for certain subjects, but do not want to make adjustments in lessons and grading	Gladly include all students with disabilities in classroom lessons, adopting a mindset that the general education classroom should be the first viable placement option with appropriate supports in place

Scores:

0–6 Reevaluate your attitude.

7–12 Much better!

12–16 Congratulations, you get it!

Great Biographies About People with Differences

Encourage students to read biographies about people with disabilities accomplishing great things in their lives. These stories will be an inspiration and teach sensitivity to all students!

Jim Abbott (baseball pitcher who was born without a right hand)

Ludwig von Beethoven (composer with deafness)

Louis Braille (created a way for people who are blind to read when he himself was blind)

Chris Burke (actor with Down syndrome)

Roy Campanella (baseball player who was paralyzed due to spinal cord injury)

Robert Dole (politician with a physical impairment)

Patty Duke (actress with a psychiatric disorder shown by manic-depressive symptoms who went public to help others realize mental illness is a disease)

Thomas Edison (inventor who probably had AD/HD)

Temple Grandin (author and entrepreneur who has autism)

Stephen Hawking (physicist with ALS-amyotrophic lateral sclerosis, otherwise known as Lou Gehrig's disease, which affects walking and speaking)

Frida Kahlo (artist who had physical difficulties, including polio)

Helen Keller (author and activist who was blind and deaf)

Juliette Gordon Low (founder of the Girl Scouts; had profound hearing loss)

Wilma Mankiller (political advocate for Cherokee Nation with muscular dystrophy)

Marlee Matlin (actress who is deaf due to childhood roseola)

Itzhak Perlman (violinist with polio who has difficulties walking and standing)

Christopher Reeve (actor with spinal cord injury who was an advocate for genetic research)

Franklin Delano Roosevelt (U.S. president with polio who hid his disability due to unaccepting public attitudes at that time)

Wilma Rudolph (Olympic athlete with a physical impairment who once couldn't even walk)

Harriet Tubman (rescuer of slaves who had epilepsy and suffered seizures)

Heather Whitestone (Miss America 1995, deaf from childhood antibiotics for influenza)

Stevie Wonder (musician who developed blindness from premature birth)

978-1-4129-5234-7

Books That Embrace Differences

The following books help students increase their exposure and sensitivity to differing abilities. After reading a book, invite students to discuss the theme and concepts with a partner or in small, cooperative groups. Invite them to share what they learned in a kind and respectful way.

16 Extraordinary Americans with Disabilities by Nancy Lobb

The Acorn People by Ron Jones (lessons learned from children with disabilities)

Al Capone Does My Shirts by Gennifer Choldenko (Autism)

Chuck Close, Up Close by Jan and Jordan Greenberg (learning and physical differences)

A Corner of the Universe by Ann M. Martin (acceptance of familial social differences)

Extraordinary People with Disabilities by Deborah Kent and Kathryn A. Quinlan

Freak the Mighty by Rodman Philbrick (physical and learning differences)

Heart Is a Lonely Hunter by Carson McCullers (cultural and hearing differences; grade 8+ reading level)

Joey Pigza Swallowed the Key by Jack Gantos (behavioral differences)

The Man Who Loved Clowns by June Rae Wood (Down's syndrome)

Millicent Min: Girl Genius by Lisa Yee (more advanced abilities)

One Step at a Time by Deborah Kent (visual differences)

Riding the Bus with My Sister: A True Life Journey by Rachel Simon (developmental differences)

Singing Hands by Delia Ray (hearing differences)

Of Sound Mind by Jean Ferris (deafness)

Stargirl by Jerry Spinelli (noncomformity)

The Survival Guide for Kids with LD: Learning Differences by Gary L. Fisher, Ph.D., and Rhonda Cummings, Ed.D.

The View from Saturday by E. L. Konigsburg (physical differences)

Parent Survey

Student's Name: _____

Parent's/Guardian's Name: _____

1. What does my child think about school?

   _____

2. What do I visualize my child doing in 10 or 15 years?

   _____

3. What are my child's special or individual needs?

   _____

4. Some words I would use to describe my child are:

   _____

5. What are my child's favorite things to do?

   _____

6. What would I change about my child's school or classroom experience?

   _____

7. What do I like about my child's school or classroom?

   _____

8. My areas of expertise that I could share with my child's class are:

   _____

9. I'd like to volunteer to help with:

   _____

10. You may contact me at:

   _____

Home: _____ Work: _____ Cell: _____

E-mail: _____

Home Address: _____

_____

Reproducible   978-1-4129-5234-7 • © Corwin Press

Charting Lessons

Use this chart to keep notes from IEPs you've read, and monitor how lessons align with modifications and goals listed in the IEP.

Subject: _____   Teachers: _____

Modifications/Accommodations	
MBHE—Modified, but high expectations	**BP**—Behavior plan
G—Grading modified	**C/T**—Computer/technology
S—Seating	**M**—Alternative materials
HW—Homework modified/reduced	**OW**—Oral/written presentations
P—Preteaching	**MS**—Multisensory techniques
R—Reteaching/repetition	**CST**—Child study team support
A—Assessment varied/simplified	**PI**—Parental involvement
SG—Study guide	**B**—Buddy system
V—Visuals	**NT**—Notetaking system
T—Extra time, or wait time for tasks	**LOV**—Learning objective varied
	O+—Other modifications

Students	Modifications/ Accommodations	Assessments/Dates Mastery Level	Comments

ABCD Quarterly Checklist of Functional Objectives

Use these codes:

A = Always
B = Becoming better
C = Can do with reminders
D = Doesn't display behavior

Student Name: _____

OBJECTIVES	Q1	Q2	Q3	Q4
Establishes eye contact with teachers and peers				
Uses proper conversational tones				
Follows classroom and school rules				
Respects authority				
Exhibits social reciprocity				
Appropriately communicates needs				
Demonstrates consistent attention during classroom lessons				
Completes all classroom assignments				
Finishes all homework and long-range assignments				
Able to take class notes independently				
Writes legibly				
Keeps an organized work area				
Respects the property of others				
Works well with groups				
Adjusts to changes in routines				
Asks for clarification when needed				
Takes pride in achievements				
Displays enthusiasm about learning				

Student Referral Planner

WHY does this student need a referral? Is it for academic, behavioral, and/or social reasons? List the student's strengths and weaknesses on the reverse side of this planner.

WHO has been contacted? Is anyone currently seeing or supporting this child?

WHEN is a good time to observe this student?

WHAT strategies/implementations have you tried? Attach any documentation such as sample academic work, tests, or behavioral logs.

Student Referral Planner
(STOP and THINK)

HOW can the CST help?

WHERE is this student currently educated?

Curriculum Recording, Documentation, and Observations

Observe and review children's progress during class lessons and chart individual modifications. For effective classroom management, this table can document progress for 10 students or record progress of one child over a period of time.

Content Area: _____

Objectives: _____

_____

Student and/ or Dates	Student is able to fully participate in the same lesson as peers.	Student needs modified expectations and/or extra materials to accomplish lesson objectives.	Student can independently participate in a different, but related assignment in the room.	Student cannot proficiently complete task in the classroom, even with support.	Brief comments, observations, needs, modifications, notes, V/A/K/T concerns, future plans

Classroom Structure to Promote Inclusion

Questions you might ask yourself

- How can teachers teach the same topic while considering different levels of development and ability?

- What about classroom management?

- Can one teacher divide the class into focused groups?

It's simple, if you think about your classroom in the following ways:

- Everyone is learning together in one room.

- Different thought processes and levels (independent, instructional, frustration) exist within the same room.

- Teaching everyone does not mean that students are learning the same breadth of material at the same time.

- The ultimate goal is progress for all based upon individual needs.

Suggestions for classroom structure

Think of how your lessons can be composed of the following three parts.

Everyone in the class could

Whole

- Listen to the same story, poem, mathematical word problem

- Look at the same picture prompt related to the content

- Chorally read or write a story together on chart paper

- Have a group discussion about the topic

- Be introduced to science and social studies vocabulary

- Preview and discuss on what skill(s) the lesson will focus (e.g., scientific method, timelines, decimals, finding the main idea, how to improve writing by substituting words)

- Be involved in a teacher demonstration or experiment, handling concrete objects or lesson-related manipulatives

Students can work with smaller groups, partners, or individually to:

Part

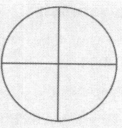

- Complete an assigned reading or writing task

- Create a product based upon what was learned (e.g., write a poem, story, or short skit; illustrate captioned pictures; solve a crossword puzzle, word search, or given problem; reenact an experiment; conduct research on the computer; read and learn more about the topic)

- Complete varying activities from a chapter, using matching colored paper (e.g. green, blue, yellow assignment) for better classroom management

- Complete learning tasks under teacher's auspices

During this time, walk around the classroom supervising or instructing smaller groups or individual students, while recording observations and individual needs evidenced.

Together the class becomes a whole unit again, while individual students, teachers, partners, and groups share:

Whole
again

- What else they learned or discovered about the topic from a book, computer, other student, teacher, or self

- A finished product created

- What they now know, giving specific details

- What they still wonder about

- Questions about the material presented

This is basically a time for all learners to celebrate their discoveries and progress with each other, while validating and reflecting upon their own learning.

Three-Question Lesson Design

Lesson design requires asking these three simple questions:

1. What are you going to teach? ⟶ Objective

2. How are you going to teach it? ⟶ Procedure

3. Did it work? ⟶ Assessment

Special education can be special for everyone involved, if you consider the following factors. Remember, not every lesson requires all of these ingredients, but perhaps being cognizant of their importance will allow these objectives to evolutionarily diffuse into the repertoires of all teachers. Think about how the following points fit into your lessons:

- Topic

- Desired Goals (Social/Academic/Emotional/Physical/Cognitive)

- Baseline Knowledge

- Motivating Activity (Visual/Auditory/Kinesthetic-Tactile Sensory Elements)

- Critical/Creative Thinking Skills

- Interpersonal Activity/Cooperative Roles

- Curriculum Connections

- Possible Accommodations

- Parallel Activity

- Anticipated roles of General Educator/Special Educator/Instructional Assistant/Student/Peers/Family/Specialists/Related Services

- Administration

- Adult/Peer/Self-Assessments

- Closure

- Revisitation Plans

Inclusive Reflections

Use this form to account for and take pride in both your own and your students' achievements and efforts. It's a speculative professional self-evaluation combined with an inclusive pedagogical student reflection. It shows where you and your students have been, where you are now, and where you are heading.

Check YES or NO to these *pedagogically ponderable* questions.

	YES	NO
Was this student's prior knowledge increased?		
Even though this student did not receive a passing grade (e.g., 50% on an evaluation), did he or she master 50% of the material?		
Do you think this student will be more proficient when he or she learns about this topic, content area, or skill again?		
Is there a way to repeat this learning and somehow individualize instruction within the classroom (e.g., alternate assignment on the same topic) if appropriate support is given, such as a parent, peer coach, or paraeducator?		
Would assigning a peer coach be beneficial to both this student and his or her student mentor?		
Can this student chart progress to take more ownership and responsibility for his or her learning?		
Is this student experiencing more accomplishments than frustrations with his or her inclusion experience in your class?		
Has physical inclusion allowed this student to develop a more positive self-image, which has translated to increased self-confidence and motivation?		
Are you experiencing personal and/or professional growth by having this student in your class?		